THE FRIENDS OF GOD

IT'S A **GREAT** NIGHT TO SAY GOOD NIGHT!

WRITTEN AND ILLUSTRATED
BY SUSAN KOVALESKI.

It's a GREAT Night to Say Good Night!

For more information or to order additional copies of this book contact:

Susan Kovaleski

skbooks67@gmail.com

ISBN: 9798819795408

Library of Congress Number: 2022909680

This book is dedicated to:
Jill: My twin sister
I love you.

David: My big brother
I love you.

Welcome, one and all!

My name is Bernadette.
I am a very kind and wise owl.

I am a friend of God,
and I love spending
time with Jesus at night
while I am awake.

SK

I am here to tell you God is just as good and big at night while you are sleeping as He is during the day while you are awake!

You don't have to be afraid!

God never leaves you.
(Deuteronomy 31:6)
God does not sleep.
(Psalm 121:4)
So you can lie down and
sleep and not be afraid.
(Psalm 3:24)

In Numbers 6:24-26,
God is praying over you,
God blesses you,
God watches over you,
God protects you,
God gives you peace.
Matthew 28:20, Jesus said
He would be with you always.

These words are promises, and God
always keeps His promises!

BECAUSE HE LOVES YOU!

What a great way to start our nighttime adventure!

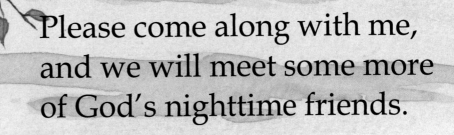

Please come along with me, and we will meet some more of God's nighttime friends.

SK

My name is Lola.

I am a beautiful
luna moth.

SV

I am very small, and I only come out at night.

Almost everything at night is bigger than me, but I know God is biggest of all!

Jesus loves me and calls me His friend.
I can trust Him to take care of me.

You can trust Jesus too!

When it's time to work, sleep, or play,
any time, night or day, say this with me:

God always loves me,
God watches over me,
God keeps me safe,
I am not afraid.
God is always with me,
God can never leave me,
God gives me peace,
I am not afraid.

My name is Donnie.

I am a kangaroo.

God made me to
jump, hop, and eat grass
mostly at night.

I like napping during
the day and keeping
busy at night.

Isn't it great that God
knows just what we need
AND what we like
any time, day or night?

When it's time to work, sleep, or play,
any time, night or day, say this with me:

God always loves me,
God watches over me,
God keeps me safe,
I am not afraid.
God is always with me,
God can never leave me,
God gives me peace,
I am not afraid.

My name is Josie.

I am a fun and funny fox. I sure like to play!

I am shy though, so nighttime is
my favorite time to play.

I am usually alone, but I am
never lonely.

I know Jesus loves me and is always with me.

Jesus loves you and is always with you too!

When it's time to work, sleep, or play,
Any time, night or day, say this with me:

God always loves me,
God watches over me,
God keeps me safe,
I am not afraid.
God is always with me,
God can never leave me,
God gives me peace,
I am not afraid.

My name is Louise.

I am a lovely armadillo.

I am little, and I sleep a lot.

God made me with armor that covers most of my body.

This armor keeps me safe, day and night.

God is so wise! He sure knew what
He was doing when He made me!

He knew what He was doing when
He made YOU too!

When it's time to work, sleep, or play,
any time, night or day, say this with me:

God always loves me,
God watches over me,
God keeps me safe,
I am not afraid.
God is always with me,
God can never leave me,
God gives me peace,
I am not afraid.

My name is Micah.

I am a very busy mouse.

At night, I am the busiest.

I love finding treasures to fill up my great big pockets.

Leaving treasures for my friends is my FAVORITE thing to do.

GIVING IS SO MUCH FUN!

I never worry because there will always be more than enough.

Jesus promises to take care of me and you.

When it's time to work, sleep, or play,
any time, night or day, say this with me:

God always loves me,
God watches over me,
God keeps me safe,
I am not afraid.
God is always with me,
God can never leave me,
God gives me peace,
I am not afraid.

My name is Hugh.

I am a koala.

God made me to eat, sleep, and live in trees.

I sleep up to 22 hours a day.

SK

So, before I go to sleep, I like to tell God thank you.

I tell Him thank you for my home, the food I eat, and the moon and stars at night.

I always thank Him for loving me and taking care of me.

I am so thankful He loves you and takes care of you too.

When it's time to work, sleep, or play,
any time, night or day, say this with me:

God always loves me,
God watches over me,
God keeps me safe,
I am not afraid.
God is always with me,
God can never leave me,
God gives me peace,
I am not afraid.

Sweet dreams to you.

My name is Ashley.

I am an aardvark.

I love to share.

During the day, I share my house with others.

Sharing is very kind.

At night, I like to pray for others. That is very kind too.

Jesus is very kind, and I want to be like Jesus.

Jesus always listens and answers when we pray. I love praying for you too.

When it's time to work, sleep, or play,
any time, night or day, say this with me:

God always loves me,
God watches over me,
God keeps me safe,
I am not afraid.
God is always with me
 God can never leave me,
God gives me peace,
I am not afraid.

My name is Patti.

I am a possum.

I am AWESOME!

I am kind, and I am a
great friend to have around.

I wake up to work and
play at night.

Even though I am small, I am not
afraid of the dark because

JESUS LOVES ME!

Jesus loves you and thinks you are
awesome too!

When it's time to work, sleep, or play,
any time, night or day, say this with me:

God always loves me,
God watches over me,
God keeps me safe,
I am not afraid.
God is always with me,
God can never leave me,
God gives me peace,
I am not afraid.

Good evening, everyone!

We are the Bullfrogs.

We have a very fun job.

We come out at night croaking and sharing with everyone!

We love to share with everyone how great and wonderful God is.

We have learned seven important truths in this book that we must share.

#1. God always loves me.

#2. God watches over me.

#3. God keeps me safe.

#4. God is always with me.

#5. God can never leave me.

#6. God gives me peace.

#7. WE ARE NOT AFRAID!

What an awesome time we've had
saying good evening to you!

We love sharing how big and good
God is with you.

Jesus sure loves you.

You can become a friend of God too.

It is so easy.

BELIEVE IN JESUS!

Ask Jesus to come and live in
your heart, and He will come
in and live with you always.

You are all invited to join us
on all of our fun adventures.

There is room for everyone!

Now it's time to say good night.

GOOD NIGHT!

See you soon.

Love,

THE FRIENDS OF GOD

SK

When you believe in Jesus and become a Friend of God:

#1. You can spend time with Jesus and become wise like Bernadette.
#2. You can know Jesus loves you and trust Him like Lola.
#3. You can know Jesus takes care of you like Donnie.
#4. You can know Jesus is always with you like Josie.
#5. You can know God keeps you safe like Louise.
#6. You can give like Micah.
#7. There is so much to be thankful for like Hugh.
#8. You can be as kind as Jesus is like Ashley.
#9. You can be safe and unafraid like Patti.
#10. You can share with everyone how GREAT God is like
     the Bullfrogs.

HOW TO BECOME A FRIEND OF GOD

1. God is love – He loves you and everyone in the whole world. (John 3:16)
2. Sin – We all sin. We do bad and wrong things. Sin keeps us separated from God. (Romans 3:23).
3. God sent His son, Jesus, so there would be no more separation between us and God. (John 3:16)
4. Jesus is the ONLY way to God. (John 14:6)
5. Jesus took all of our sin and died on the cross. (Romans 5:8; John 15:13)
6. Jesus was dead for three days, and God raised Him from the dead. Now Jesus is ALIVE! (Matthew 28:5-6)
7. Now sin can no longer separate us from God. (Romans 8:38-39)
8. You must believe that Jesus died and rose again in order to become a Friend of God. (Romans 10:9-10)

If you believe these things and want to pray with me, say this with me:

God, thank You for loving me and for sending Jesus to die on the cross and take my sin away. I am sorry for my sins. Jesus, I believe You died for me and rose again. Please come into my heart. Thank You for making me like You, for loving me, and never leaving me.

YOU ARE NOW A FRIEND OF GOD!

ABOUT THE AUTHOR

Author and illustrator, Susan Kovaleski loves to put pen to paper to see what will appear. Her love for creation inspires her artwork and her life.

Susan grew up in Gillette, Wyoming but now lives in Oldsmar, Florida with her son, Gregory, and enjoys her daily walks with her dog, Layla.

Other Books by
Susan Kovaleski